ISBN 978-1-333-71439-0
PIBN 10538436

This book is a reproduction of an important historical work. Forgotten Books uses
state-of-the-art technology to digitally reconstruct the work, preserving the original format
whilst repairing imperfections present in the aged copy. In rare cases, an imperfection in
the original, such as a blemish or missing page, may be replicated in our edition. We do,
however, repair the vast majority of imperfections successfully; any imperfections that
remain are intentionally left to preserve the state of such historical works.

English
Français
Deutsche
Italiano
Español
Português

www.forgottenbooks.com

Mythology Photography **Fiction**
Fishing Christianity **Art** Cooking
Essays Buddhism Freemasonry
Medicine **Biology** Music **Ancient
Egypt** Evolution Carpentry Physics
Dance Geology **Mathematics** Fitness
Shakespeare **Folklore** Yoga Marketing
Confidence Immortality Biographies
Poetry **Psychology** Witchcraft
Electronics Chemistry History **Law**
Accounting **Philosophy** Anthropology
Alchemy Drama Quantum Mechanics
Atheism Sexual Health **Ancient History**
Entrepreneurship Languages Sport
Paleontology Needlework Islam
Metaphysics Investment Archaeology
Parenting Statistics Criminology
Motivational

Grace Before Meals

✠

BRIEF PRAYERS

ARRANGED FOR EACH DAY IN THE YEAR

COMPILED BY

A. WILLIAM NYCE

AND

HUBERT BUNYEA

✠

THE JOHN C. WINSTON CO.
PHILADELPHIA

Foreword

✠

IT is customary in most households, where the family spirit recognizes the kindness of God in guarding the lives and souls of His people, to pause for a moment before the meal at which the family is gathered together and have offered a simple prayer of thanks to our Father in Heaven for His provision of the means by which we live. This little act of devotion, simple as it may appear, doubtless has kept pure and holy the spirits of untold millions, to whom its observance is both an act of sincere gratitude and a gentle but powerful reminder of the constant relation between Our Lord and His children.

Yet, if the form of grace which is spoken has been used over and over again in the same family, it is not unlikely that it may become merely a matter of form and lose much of its meaning and helpfulness from the monotony of constant repetition; or, if the speaker tries to relieve this monotony by searching out fresh texts or to compose suitable brief prayers, he may at times have difficulty in finding appropriate words in which to express the feelings of his family on these occasions.

There is also a large number of homes in which the gentle tribute of grace before meals is often neglected, or has not perhaps been customary, although the atmosphere may be really religious and a strong desire prevail to keep it so. Possibly the person who should lead the thoughts of his little circle in these lines has his mind on objects of material necessity and does not find it easy to give voice to the convictions which really lie deep in his heart.

And there are too many other dwellings where the spirit of thankfulness to God but rarely makes itself heard, although there may be within their walls young children or others to whom a few moments daily spent in devotion would mean a gain in goodness and in character.

This little book has been prepared for the home circle, in the hope that it may encourage reverence and gratitude by supplying appropriate graces to be spoken before meals at which the family meets together, and to provide a pleasing variety of form with special prayers for national feast-days without doctrinal or denominational allusions.

In preparing and arranging these pages the editors have spared no pains to make a book that will be practical and useful. Valuable suggestions gleaned from many sources have been incorporated. It is not the product of one mind, but rather the assembled expressions of many devout servants of God, and this book as it goes forth on its mission is also an answer to numerous requests that such a volume be given to the public.

January

January 1.   Morning

New Year's

As we gather around the festive board this beautiful New Year's Day, we thank Thee dear Lord for Thy goodness to us, and pray God the hungry everywhere may be fed. Be with us during this day, guide and keep us, we ask in His name.   Amen.

January 1.   Noonday

New Year's Prayer

O God, our good desires fulfil;
   The bad do Thou restrain;
Reveal to us Thy Holy Will,
   And make our duty plain.

Sustain us by Thy heavenly grace
   And all our needs supply,
Help us to run the heavenly race
   With Jesus ever nigh.   Amen.

9

January 1. Evening

We ask Heaven's blessing to descend on the food which is before us. May this New Year find us more willing to do Thy bidding, for Christ's sake. Amen.

✠

January 2

For the continuance of Thy loving kindness unto us, we give Thee all thanks, O Lord. Fulfil all our needs and save us, for Jesus' sake. Amen.

✠

January 3

For every gift of nature and of grace, for our heavenly vision of Thee, for all blessings within and without, for all that Thy love has yet in store for us, O God, we give Thee gracious thanks. Through Christ Jesus. Amen.

January 4

Thou knowest what things we have need of, even before we ask Thee. In Thy mercy behold our present wants and be ever gracious unto Thy servants, for Christ's sake. Amen.

✠

January 5

Wherein we have done amiss, we humbly crave Thy forgiveness, O Father in Heaven. Draw near to us now and overshadow us with Thy great goodness, for Jesus' sake. Amen.

✠

January 6

O God let all the world bless Thee, for there is none without the token of Thy favor. We, the children of Thy love, rejoice to acknowledge Thy goodness. Grant that we may of Thy mercy inherit the eternal blessedness of Heaven. Amen.

January 7

Make us slow to forget Thee, O God, as we have reason to remember Thee constantly. Hast Thou not supplied all our wants? In all that Thou dost for us, may Thy holy name be glorified. Amen.

✠

January 8

Every creature, O God, is the recipient of Thy grace. Make us all more thankful to Thee, and help us to praise and serve Thee, for Thy name's sake. Amen.

✠

January 9

In Thy great love, dear Lord, Thou didst go through the shadows and the gloom and the agony of Mount Calvary, in order that we might know the brightness, the gladness, the glory of Paradise. Through all our lives Thy ` love has never failed us, and we would commemorate it again as we are gathered around this table of Thy bounty. Amen.

January 10

Thou hast saved and preserved us, O Lord, and may we by our lives never bring reproach upon the name of Jesus, but ever learn to live for Thee, and to Thy honor. Amen.

✠

January 11

We thank Thee, Father, for the measure of health and strength we have, wherewith to do our daily work and to serve Thee. Keep us healthful, useful and faithful, for the Christ's sake. Amen.

✠

January 12

When all Thy mercies, O my God!
　My rising soul surveys,
Transported with the view, I'm lost
　In wonder, love and praise.
Ten thousand thousand precious gifts
　Our daily thanks employ.
Nor is the least a cheerful heart
　That tastes those gifts with joy. Amen.

January 13

All and more than all we need, O Lord, Thou hast given to us. May we ever thank Thee humbly and serve Thee willingly. Save us from all sin. Amen.

✠

January 14

Lord, wilt Thou never cease Thy kindly care over us, and may we also continue unceasingly to bless Thee for all Thy past and present blessings. Amen.

✠

January 15

God, be merciful unto us, and bless us, and make Thy face to shine upon us, that Thy way may be known upon earth, Thy saving health among all nations. Then shall the earth yield her increase, and God, even our own God, shall bless us. Amen.

January 16

Teach us, Jesus, that as we have done unto the least of Thy brethren we have done unto Thee. Grant that this food may strengthen us in body and mind to serve Thee by doing good unto our fellowmen. Amen.

✠

January 17

We are bound to Thee, O Lord, by the ties of a great love. May that love lead us into the paths of duty, that as Thou hast done mercifully unto us, so may we ever try to be worthy of Thee. Amen.

✠

January 18

Blessed be the Lord for all his mercies, for giving us food to eat and raiment to wear, and for delivering us from many evils which our sins have justly deserved. We thank Thee, especially, O Lord, for the gift of Jesus Christ, Thy Son, for whose sake we pray Thee to pardon our offences, and to receive our souls. Amen.

January 19

Do Thou bless our meal to-day, and may Thy Spiritual Presence fill us with gratitude for all these abundant blessings.   Amen.

✠

January 20

Grant, Lord, to provide clothing and shelter for the poor this day.   Feed the hungry, and soothe the sick.   May Thy Spirit of Good fill all our hearts as we receive of Thee.   We give Thee every thanks.   Amen.

✠

January 21

Let us with a gladsome mind,
Praise the Lord for he is kind:
All things living he doth feed;
His full hand supplies their need:
For his mercies shall endure,
Ever faithful, ever sure.   Amen.

January 22

Give us grace to be grateful for the blessings which Thou hast so bountifully spread before us to-day. In Thine own name. Amen.

✠

January 23

O Thou who satisfiest our mouths with the good things, we praise Thee for Thy gracious providence, and invoke Thy blessing as we partake. Amen.

✠

January 24

Again, Lord, Thou hast shown forth Thy mighty love in providing us this food. May we devote its sustaining power to the cause for which Thou wouldst have us labor. Bless all that is undertaken for Thee, in Jesus' name. Amen.

January 25

O Lord, we thank Thee for these mercies and the food laid before us. Help us to realize Thy great favors to us and let our health and strength be devoted to Thy work. Amen.

✠

January 26

We give Thee thanks, for life and all its blessings. Give Thou this food to nourish our bodies, and Thy Word of Truth to sustain our souls. Amen.

✠

January 27

While satisfying our physical hunger and thirst, grant us, Lord, to have that more blessed Hunger and Thirst after righteousness. Protect us from unworthy desires and ambitions. Show us what is Thy gracious will for us, and accept all our thanks. Amen.

January 28

What is Man, O Lord, that Thou art mindful of him? And yet we give Thee thanks that we are the constant objects of all Thy love and watchcare. Amen.

✠

January 29

We thank Thee, O Lord, for the food provided us each day and we pray that it shall strengthen our love for Thee and give us the spirit to enter into Thy work. Amen.

✠

January 30

We need no greater proof of Thy love than the blessings Thou dost continually shower upon us. The sunshine and the rain both in their own way minister to us. So also do joy and sorrow, if in the midst of them we have the faith to remember Thee. Grant us this faith, for Christ's sake. Amen.

Thou hast dealt kindly with us, Heavenly Father, in giving the grace of comfort. We rejoice in the privilege of acknowledging all again unto Thee with thanksgiving. Amen.

February

February 1

The earth is the Lord's and the fullness thereof. We praise Thy holy name that out of Thy plenty Thou hast so well remembered our necessities. Amen.

✠

February 2

Lord, Thou hast been our dwelling place. Supply our need. Pardon all our past wrongs, and grant that the rest of our days may be such that we may have no fear of the Great Beyond. In the Saviour's name we ask it. Amen.

✠

February 3

Almighty God, Thou art the Source and Fountain of all our benefits. We are truly thankful for these blessings, and pray that Thou wilt crown them with Thy spiritual presence. Amen.

February 4

We give Thee thanks, O Lord, for the material comforts we do this day enjoy, and for spiritual comforts which exceed all the delights of the world.   Amen.

☩

February 5

Help us, O Lord, to rejoice and be glad in this the Day that Thou hast made.   We praise Thee for Thy bountiful provisions for our bodies and souls. Strengthen and upbuild us this day, and make us like unto Thyself. Amen.

☩

February 6

Holy Father, give us this day our daily bread.   May we appropriate to its proper use the food before us, and render ever unto Thee the thanks that are Thine.   In Christ's name. Amen.

February 7

Keep us ever humble, Lord, that we may be the ready recipients of Thy goodness. Deliver us from pride and wickedness, and supply our wants. Amen.

✠

February 8

Once more, O Christ, we are reminded that Thou dost never forget Thine own. In loving providence, Thou art the same yesterday and to-day and forever. We magnify Thy great name, and pray Thine aid continually. Amen.

✠

February 9

Thou knowest, O Lord, what things we have need of before we ask Thee. All the blessings that we receive do constantly remind us of Thy unfailing love for us. We give Thee all praise. Amen.

February 10

Thy mercies, O Heavenly Father, are new each day and we pray Thee that Thou wilt constantly renew us in strength of body and spirit to serve Thee acceptably.   Amen.

✠

February 11

In the strength of this food give unto us continuance of life, O God, that we may be spared longer to permeate with the spirit of Jesus, this world in which we live.   To His blessed name be glory and honor, forever. Amen.

✠

February 12

We do thank Thee, O God, for the measure of blessing Thou hast been pleased to bestow upon us, and that Thou, who art the possessor of every good thing, art not forgetful of our present need.   Amen.

February 13

O Lord, our God, in Thee do we put our trust. Renew from day to day these present favors, and give us faith ever to accept Thy gifts with grateful hearts. Amen.

✠

February 14

Like as a father pitieth his children, so, O Lord, Thou lovest them that fear Thee. It is with childlike trust we look unto Thee this day for the food we so constantly are in need of, and Thou art so constant in providing. Amen.

✠

February 15

Thou that forgettest not the cry of the humble, we praise Thee for the mercies of this hour, and implore that Thou wilt give unto us to be ever grateful for Thy love. Amen.

February 16

As our Lord Jesus has taught us by His word and His example, we give Thee thanks, our Father, for the meat and drink that Thou hast given for our bodily sustenance.   Amen.

✠

February 17

Bless the Lord, O my Soul, and forget not all His benefits, Who healeth all thy diseases, Who forgiveth all thine iniquities, Who satisfieth thy mouth with good things, Who crowneth thee with loving kindness.   Amen.

✠

February 18

O Lord, we thank Thee for life and the joy of living, for health and strength, and for these blessings fresh from Thine hand of love. Through Jesus Christ.   Amen.

February 19

Lord, Thou art our Shepherd, we shall not want, give us peace and blessing. Refresh our bodies. Restore our souls. Lead us in the paths of the righteous for Thy name's sake. Amen.

✠

February 20

Our Heavenly Father, give us grateful hearts for this, an expression of Thy great love for us, bless this food to the nourishment of our bodies, take away our sins, and finally own and crown us Thine in Heaven, for Christ's sake. Amen.

✠

February 21

Lord, Thou art not far from every one of us, and moment by moment we have reason to acknowledge Thy nearness because of these, Thy constant blessings. Amen.

February 22

We thank Thee, O God, for the memory of
him whose birth we celebrate to-day. We
thank Thee that Thou didst give to this man
the broad vision and the mighty inspiration
that was able to lead our nation to independence. Continue Thy guiding of our rulers,
that all may have the courage and foresight
to work out Thy mighty purposes in this Thy
promised land of freedom. The glory shall be
Thine. Amen.

✠

February 23

Thou art the living God, near to Thy human
creatures, and the same forevermore. Accept
our thanks for this daily revelation of Thy
love and nearness. Amen.

February 24

Dear Lord, let it be our earnest prayer to serve Thee better day by day as we grow in grace and trust to Thee for our wants in soul and body. Bless our humble home, where we trust Thee all and in all, and where Thou hast given bountifully to such as would receive Thee. Amen.

✠

February 25

For these and all His blessings, God's Holy name be praised, for Christ's sake. Amen.

✠

February 26

All things come of Thee, O Lord, and for these and all Thy blessings we give hearty thanks in the name of Christ our Redeemer. Amen.

February 27

O Lord, our most gracious Heavenly Father, bless these Thy gifts which we are about to receive from Thy bountiful fold.   Bless each one of us, and look upon us in mercy, in the sweet name of Jesus our Saviour.   Amen.

✠

February 28

Bless, O Lord, this provision of Thy goodness to our use, and us to Thy service for Christ's sake.   Amen.

✠

February 29

Bless, O Lord, this food to our use, and us in Thy service; through Jesus Christ our Lord. Amen.

March

March 1

Thanks be to Thee, O Lord, for these and all the blessings so generously provided. We thank Thee in the name of Christ. Amen.

✠

March 2

We give Thee thanks, O Heavenly Father, for our food which Thou dost provide for us. Our thanksgiving could never measure up to Thy gifts, but we pray Thee to make us all more conscious of Thy blessed goodness, and help us to know Thyself; we ask it in Jesus' name. Amen.

✠

March 3

Lord, we thank Thee for this food. Sanctify it to our use, pardon our sins and save us, for Christ's sake. Amen.

March 4

For the food of which we are about to partake, we thank Thee, O Lord, in Christ's name. Amen.

✠

March 5

Our Heavenly Father, bless us as we are about to partake of this our food which Thou dost give each one of us. Teach us to know more the meaning of these words, "Give us this day our daily bread," and to be more grateful to Thee, in Christ Jesus' name. Amen.

✠

March 6

O dear Heavenly Father, who lookest down upon us in mercy and pitying love, we do thank Thee for our daily repast from Thine earthly store, for our burden is light with Thy grace. Amen.

March 7

O God, Thy mercies are fresh every day and call forth each day anew our voices of thanksgiving. Through Jesus Christ. Amen.

✠

March 8

Father in heaven, look upon our table and bless this which Thou hast been so good to provide for us; bless each one of us gathered here and teach us to be more thankful to Thee. We ask it in Thy precious name, O Jesus. Amen.

✠

March 9

O Lord, make us thankful for this food which we are about to receive for the nourishment of our bodies. Continue Thy mercies unto us, O Lord, and save us, through Christ our Redeemer. Amen.

March 10

We thank Thee, our Heavenly Father, for these Thy good gifts. Bless them to our use, sanctify us and save us for Christ's sake. Amen.

March 11

Thou Giver of every good gift, we acknowledge our unworthiness to partake of Thy grace, but give Thee thanks that Thou hast not measured Thy blessing according to our deserts. Give us strength to employ every blessing to Thy name's honor and glory. Amen.

March 12

O Lord, as Thou didst sanctify with Thy sweet presence the home of Mary and Martha and Lazarus, we ask Thee to be the guest at our table to-day, and bless this meal. Amen.

March 13

Our Father Who art in Heaven, we do thank Thee for all Thy kindnesses to us. As Thou hast given us this bread, help us to give Thee our service, for Jesus' sake. Amen.

✠

March 14

As Thou hast increased our blessing and joy from day to day, O Lord, so do Thou increase also our measure of love and gratitude to Thee for these, Thy tender mercies. Amen.

✠

March 15

O Lord, may the mercies and love Thou showest us be continued unto us each day, that we may have the strength and courage to acknowledge Thy great gifts and enter into Thy work with the determination to see its greater success. Accept our thanks for this provision of food and save our souls from sin, for Christ sake. Amen.

March 16

We thank Thee, Lord, for Thy thought of us, so kind and so untiring. Thou hast prepared for us these blessings we now receive. May the hours before us be spent in gratitude to Thee. In Thy name. Amen.

✠

March 17

Almighty giver of Good, we thank Thee for Thy loving kindness to us. Thou openest Thy hand, and we are fed. Be at this table we pray Thee, and bless our gathering together. In His name. Amen.

✠

March 18

For these blessings received from Thy hand of Love, O Lord, we offer our thanks, beseeching Thee that we may continue to enjoy the life Thou gavest, and use our health and strength for the furtherance of Thy great work. Amen.

March 19

When we eat or drink, may we do all to Thy praise, O God. May the food before us refresh our frail mortal bodies, and may we be good stewards of Thy bounty. For Thy name's sake. Amen.

✠

March 20

May Thy sanctifying presence be with us in the breaking of bread. Enable us to commune with Thee through these and all blessings, and make us more obedient, and more Christlike. Amen.

✠

March 21

O God, our Help and our Deliverer; without Thee we are poor and needy, but we give Thee thanks that through Thy aid, all our wants are filled. Amen.

March 22

Lord, Thou dost give us strength through this food. We thank Thee that we may go forth in the strength of the Lord God to do the tasks that yet lie before us. Through the Christ. Amen.

✠

March 23

Thou, O Lord, art our strong habitation whereunto we may continually resort, and unto Thee we look in faith for this day's bread. Amen.

✠

March 24

As Thou providest food for our bodies each day, O Lord, feed our hungry souls with Thy Spirit that we may not perish, that we may have the joy of everlasting life, and that by the strength Thou givest us we may be able to save some poor soul from sin. Amen.

March 25

O Lord, our flesh and our heart faileth, but Thou art our portion of strength forever. Make us worthy to-day to approach the board laden with these tokens of Thy love.   Amen.

✠

March 26

O Thou Shepherd of Israel, our cup runneth over with Thy goodness to us.   Help us to be worthy of all these favors, and may we use them in glorifying Thee.   In the Saviour's name.   Amen.

✠

March 27

Lord, we acknowledge that these gifts are the gifts of Thy great love to us.   Thou couldst not but give unto us, for Thou art Love Thyself.   We praise Thee for what Thou art, and for all that Thou hast done, through Christ our Saviour.   Amen.

March 28

Our Father, we ask Thee to bless the food before us to our physical needs, and feed our spirits with Thy truth, for Jesus' sake.   Amen.

✠

March 29

Father in Heaven, we will hope continually in Thee and praise Thee more and more for Thy loving providence and these present blessings.   Through Jesus Christ.   Amen.

✠

March 30

May we be always conscious O Lord, of the love and mercies shown us through Thy provision for our weak souls and bodies.   Thou replenisheth the fount from which we daily draw our supplies.   Let us not overlook that Spirit of love Thou giveth us each day, but let us be as regular in drawing that important provision as those which sustain the body. Accept our humble thanks and save our souls from sin, for Jesus' sake.   Amen.

Our Father, wilt Thou bless this food for our bodies and feed our souls with the "Bread of Life?" We ask in Jesus' name. Amen.

✠

Easter

This day, O Christ, we celebrate Thy victory over death. Bring to us new life of body through this nourishment, and new life of soul by Thy presence with us now and help us to say with Thy servant of old, "Thanks be to God which giveth us the victory through Jesus Christ our Lord." Amen.

April

April 1

Our Father, we thank Thee for our daily bread and ask that we may serve Thee with the strength gained from it.   Amen.

✠

April 2

O Merciful Father, we come to Thee in humbleness to thank Thee for these provisions, which Thou art constantly providing.   We do thank Thee, O Lord, and pray that Thy Spirit will bring us to a greater realization of Thy love and that we shall work more faithfully in Thy cause.   Accept our thanks for this food and save our souls from sin, for Christ's sake.   Amen.

✠

April 3

Our heavenly Father, we pray Thee to grant Thy blessings upon these gifts of Thy providence and as we live upon Thy bounty may we live to Thy glory, through Christ our Saviour.   Amen.

April 4

Father we thank Thee for this food,
  For all the blessings thou dost give.
Strengthen our bodies and our souls,
  And let us for Thy service live.   Amen.

✠

April 5

O Saviour, as we come again to Thy table
and the food Thou hast so lovingly provided
we pray for those less fortunate, those whom
illness and misfortune have visited and those
in sin.   Provide, O Merciful Saviour, for them
as Thou hast provided for us.   Teach us tha
we should show unto our fellow-man mercy
and justice, and never let us pass by an opportunity when we may do good to them and
thus serve Thee.   Amen.

✠

April 6

Our Father, we bless Thee for this food and
for all the expressions of Thy goodness to us
Give us grace to do Thy will, we pray through
faith in Jesus Christ our Lord.   Amen.

April 7

Our Heavenly Father, we thank Thee for all Thy mercies. Give the sanctified use of this food and forgive our sins we ask through Christ our Saviour. Amen.

✠

April 8

O Heavenly Father, Thou who furnisheth us with our daily bread, who forgiveth our sins, who feedeth us from His hand and our souls from His Spirit, accept our thanks for this, another manifestation of Thy great love. Help us to enter into Thy work and spread the Gospel, and save us from sin, for Christ's sake. Amen.

✠

April 9

Almighty Father, we give Thee thanks for the blessings conferred upon us, so weak and so sinful. Give us the strength to abide by Thy will, forgive us our sins and bring us to eternal life. Amen.

April 10

O God, Thou hast taught us to lift our eyes unto the hills, from whence cometh our help. Our help cometh from Thee who madest Heaven and Earth. To Thee we render thanks for all Thy good. Amen.

✠

April 11

With grateful hearts, O Lord, we accept these Thy gifts, and those which Thou art constantly giving. Help us that we may be always grateful, that we shall avoid temptations, that should we encounter them we may have the strength and courage to resist, but should we fall into sin, lift us out of its depths and forgive us, O Lord. Accept our thanks for this food, and bring us to everlasting life. Amen.

✠

April 12

These further blessings which Thou dost give us, O Lord, show that the Shepherd forgets not His sheep. May we be always worthy of Thy love. Amen.

April 13

We implore Thee, Heavenly Father, to accept our humble thanks for this food. Teach us to use it rightly and to Thy service. Forgive us our sins and save us, for Christ's sake. Amen.

✠

April 14

Merciful Saviour, who by Thy suffering and death on the cross hast paid its price of all our sins, we praise Thee this day and implore Thy constant mercy and providing care, for Thy holy name's sake. Amen.

✠

April 15

Let Thy peace and blessing descend upon us as we take of Thy bounty. Fill our hearts with love and praise unto Him Who doeth all things well. Amen.

April

April 16

Lord, make us truly grateful for the blessings of this day, and keep us Thine evermore. Amen.

✠

April 17

Lord, Thou art so merciful unto us. If, in our weakness, our Saviour, we have shown ourselves to be ungrateful, pardon us for that failing, strengthen us that we may be always conscious of Thy love and help us to be better that we may enjoy the everlasting life promised us. Accept our humble thanks for this food, and save us from sin, for Christ's sake. Amen.

✠

April 18

Thou dost provide for us with a bountiful hand, O Lord. May we always be humbly thankful for Thy mercies and serve Thee with willing hearts. Save us from sin and keep us always grateful for Thy love. Amen.

April 19

O Lord, the great mercies received at Thy hands prove to us Thy great love for Thy children. Accept our humble gratitude for all Thy favors, for this provision of food, and save us for Christ's sake. Amen.

✠

April 20

This food, which Thou dost place before us, we are grateful for, O Lord. Help us that we may never forget our duty to Thee, that we may work for the advancement of Thy work and help those to see who do not. Forgive us our sins and save our souls for Christ's sake. Amen.

✠

April 21

We give Thee thanks, Almighty God, our Heavenly Father, for this which Thou hast prepared for us. Bless, O Lord, these Thy gifts which we are about to receive from Thy bountiful fold, for Christ's sake. Amen.

April 22

O Lord, we are truly grateful for the food before us. Renew from day to day the mercies shown us in the past and grant our prayer to make our lives better and our faith and love for Thee stronger. Amen.

✠

April 23

O Lord, we thank Thee for this food. We pray that Thou wilt provide for the poor and the hungry and the sinner that they may realize how great is Thy love and care. Help us that we may help others, and save our souls, for Christ's sake. Amen.

✠

April 24

We accept, O God, Thy mercy and grace. Wilt Thou help us to show in our daily lives our gratitude for Thy kindness. Through Jesus Christ our Lord. Amen.

April 25

Lord Jesus, continue to bless us, and make us thankful for this food and for all Thy past and present blessings. Amen.

✠

April 26

Make us a grateful people, O Father, for Thy provision for us. Help us always to remember our duty—that of helping others to see Thy unwavering love for Thy children. Accept our thanks for this provision of food and forgive us our sins. Amen.

✠

April 27

Make us thankful, O Lord, for health and strength to receive the blessings Thou hast provided for us. Amen.

April 28

When partaking of Thy numerous blessings, may we never forget to give Thee our thanks for the daily gifts we receive at Thy hand. Grant that all things may be to our good and Thy glory, for Jesus' sake.   Amen.

✠

April 29

Thy great love, O Lord, has taught us our duty to Thee.   Help us that we may perform it and not stray into the paths of sin.   We have been so bountifully provided for that we can not fail to come to Thee in the acceptance of this food which Thou hast again provided, and thank Thee with grateful hearts and pray that we may always try to be worthy of Thy love.   Amen.

✠

April 30

Heavenly Father great and good,
We thank Thee for this daily food.
Bless us even as we pray;
Guide and keep us through this day.   Amen.

May

May 1

Heavenly Father, we give Thee thanks for the many benefits we receive at Thy hands. Bless all Thy creatures of earth, and receive us at last in Heaven with Thee, for Jesus' sake. Amen.

May 2

Our Father Who art in Heaven, we thank Thee for the protection granted to each one of us during the past night. Be with us now and bless this food to the use of our temporal bodies. Feed our souls with the Bread of Life, pardon all our sins and save us for Christ's sake. Amen.

May 3

Heavenly Father, we thank Thee for all Thy blessings and mercies. Continue to bless us as Thou seest we need; we ask for Jesus' sake. Amen.

May 4

We give Thee thanks, O Lord, for Thy providing love, and for the power that is ours to partake thereof. Amen.

✠

May 5

O Lord, Thou didst create the earth for man, and gave him the fruits of the earth and of the flocks and herds for his support, and hast said that our food is to be sanctified by prayer. Sanctify this food to us, and us to Thy service for Jesus' sake. Amen.

✠

May 6

O Lord, how can we thank Thee for the continued mercies received at Thy hands. Each day we have cause to be profoundly grateful unto Thee. Accept our thanks, O Lord, for the great mercies Thou art constantly showing us, and help us to live a good and useful life and to be ever grateful for Thy mercies and love. Amen.

May 7

Thy great love is again manifested, O Lord, in this provision of food. May we use the health and strength it giveth us through Thy Grace, in the cause for which Thou wouldst have us work. May we be further enlightened as to Thy teachings and enlighten others of Thy work. Save us for Christ's sake. Amen.

✠

May 8

O Lord, all creatures wait upon Thee that they may receive their good. Thou openest Thy hands and they are filled with good. Help us to remember always that we are dependent on Thee and with thankfulness partake of the food before us, for Jesus' sake. Amen.

✠

May 9

O God, we thank Thee for these temporal gifts. Help us to remember the greatest gift of all, Thy Son Jesus. Amen.

May 10

Heavenly Father, we thank Thee for all that Thy love supplies, and for this Thy daily blessing. May we show our gratitude to Thee by serving Thee wholly. Amen.

✠

May 11

For all Thy favors to us, Father, we have in the past been slow in our appreciation and gratitude. We realize more and more from Thy continued mercies the love Thou hast for us. Help us to be more appreciative, and to become more identified with Thy service. Give us our daily bread and forgive us our sins, for Christ's sake. Amen.

✠

May 12

For these continued blessings we thank Thee, O Lord. Save us all for Christ's sake. Amen.

Day 13

Accept our thanks, O Heavenly Father, for these mercies before us. Bless them for their intended use and save us for Christ's sake. Amen.

✠

Day 14

At this hour, as we break the bread of life, we feel our need of Thee, O Father in heaven. Thou hast given the increase, and we partake thereof. For all that Thou hast done, we return our sincere thanks. Amen.

✠

Day 15

O Lord, every good and perfect gift cometh from Thee. Accept our thanks for this food and may we devote our lives to Thee in return for Thy goodness, through Jesus Christ our Lord. Amen.

May 16

Accept our thanks, Heavenly Father, for these and all other blessings for Jesus' sake. Amen.

✠

May 17

Receive, we pray Thee, our gratitude, feed all mankind, we pray Thee, as Thou hast fed us. Deliver us from evil, and the effects of evil. And when Thou art done with us here on earth, own and receive us into Thy kingdom above, we ask in Thy name. Amen.

✠

May 18

Our Father, we thank Thee for this expression of Thy loving kindness to us. Guide us by Thy Spirit into all truth and bring us to Thyself in Heaven, through Jesus Christ our Lord. Amen.

May 19

Our Heavenly Father, we pray Thee to accept our thanks for the blessings before us which are an expression of Thy constant love and care. Sanctify them to us and us to Thy service, for Jesus' sake. Amen.

✠

May 20

Accept our heartfelt thanks, our Father, for the food Thou hast spread before us and pardon our sins for Christ's sake. Amen.

✠

May 21

Our Heavenly Father, we acknowledge that every good and perfect gift cometh from Thee. Now, unto Thee do we return most hearty thanks for these material gifts. Strengthen us by them, that we may have life to use for the glory of Thy kingdom in doing service for Thee. And unto Thee be all honor, now and forevermore. Amen.

May 22

We thank Thee, our Father, for what Thou hast so bountifully provided for us to sustain our perishing bodies. Sanctify it to our good and our souls to Thy service for Christ's sake. Amen.

✠

May 23

We thank Thee, our Father in heaven, for health and strength, for life and opportunity for service. Break unto us day by day the bread of life. Cleanse us from sin, and all secret faults and evil desires. Renew in us day by day right spirits, pure motives and unto Thee be all glory, all honor, for propagating life which Thou hast begun in us. Give us our daily bread, as Thou seest we need. In Thy name. Amen.

✠

May 24

Our Father, Who art in heaven, bless the provisions of Thy bounty now set before us, and for our souls the bread of life, in Christ's name. Amen.

May 25

We thank Thee, our Father, for this, another manifestation of Thy loving kindness toward us. Bless this food we are to partake of to the use of our bodies and forgive us our sins, for Christ's sake. Amen.

✠

May 26

Our Father Who art in heaven, we would not partake of these bounties without returning most hearty thanks to Thee, from whom the earth receives her increase. Thou hast supplied us with the bounties of life, for which our hearts go out in thankfulness to Thee. Bless, we pray Thee, these provisions to the nourishment of our bodies, and ourselves to Thy service. Amen.

✠

May 27

Bless us, O Lord, and these Thy gifts, which we are about to receive from Thy bounty. Through Christ our Lord. Amen.

May 28

Sanctify, O Lord, we beseech Thee, this food to our use, and us to Thy service and make us truly thankful for all these mercies, through Christ our Lord. Amen.

✠

May 29

Unto Thee, Father, Son and Holy Spirit do we return most hearty thanks for the many blessings that we receive at Thy hand, and especially for the provisions now set before us. Do Thou bless them to the nourishment of our bodies, and to the nourishment of our souls. We acknowledge that all good cometh from Thee and all true blessings of life. In Thy name. Amen.

May 30

Memorial Day

O God, we thank Thee that Thou hast preserved us a nation with liberty and justice. Help us this day to honor the men who fought and died for our Union. May we realize how nearly the spirit of patriotism is to Thine own great Heart, and may we serve Thee the better for the memories of to-day. Amen.

✠

May 31

It is with grateful hearts that we thank Thee, O God, for this daily manna Thou hast provided for our frail bodies. Forgive our many sins for Jesus' sake. Amen.

June

June 4

Our Father, who art in heaven, we are gathered together here in Thy holy name. Bless this of which we are about to partake; save us and fit us for Thy heavenly home, through our Lord and Saviour Jesus Christ. Amen.

✠

June 5

We thank Thee, Heavenly Father, that Thou hast so graciously supplied our returning wants. Continue, we pray Thee, to be our God and Keeper, supply the wants of the destitute, and fill the earth with Thy glory, for Christ's sake. Amen.

✠

June 6

Dear Father, recognizing Thee as the Giver of all good and perfect gifts, we do thank Thee for the gift of daily bread. Grant that we may be found worthy to partake of this blessed food, pardon our numberless sins, and save us at last in glory. Amen.

June 7

Dear Jesus, we rejoice that it is ours to offer up our thanks for this food placed before us; food to strengthen the body and nourish the soul. Consecrate our lives more fully to Thy service, we ask in Thy name. Amen.

✠

June 8

The eyes of all wait upon Thee, and Thou givest them their meat in due season. Thou openest Thy hand, and satisfiest the desire of every living being. O Lord God, Heavenly Father, bless unto us these Thy gifts, which by Thy tender kindness Thou hast bestowed upon us through Jesus Christ, our Lord. Amen.

✠

June 9

We thank Thee, O God, for this food before us, for the nourishment of our bodies. May we be as faithful in serving Thee as Thou art in providing our daily bread. These things we ask for Jesus' sake. Amen.

June 10

Lord, we would ask Thy blessing on this food; bless it to the good of our bodies that we may be better prepared for the battles of life, for Christ's sake, we ask it. Amen.

✠

June 11

O God, as we are assembled once again to partake of this daily provided food, knowing it is the work of Thy hands, how gratefully our hearts yield thanks! Teach us how to work, and how to live, and how to serve Thee more faithfully; in Thy name we ask it. Amen.

✠

June 12

Lord, we bless Thee for these and all Thy mercies. Be gracious toward us and forgive our sins, we ask in Christ's name. Amen.

June 13

Accept the gratitude of our hearts, our Father, for these mercies. May we prove ourselves worthy of all Thy benefits through Jesus Christ our Lord. Amen.

✠

June 14

To Thee, O Lord, our hearts we raise,
    For mercies marking all our days.
Each morn our wants are satisfied
    With food Thy love and care provide. Amen.

✠

June 15

We give Thee thanks, O Almighty God, for all Thy mercies. Who livest and reignest world without end. Amen.

June 16

Be present at our table, Lord;
Be here and everywhere adored.
These creatures bless, and grant that we
May feast in Paradise with Thee.   Amen.

✠

June 17

O God our Father and our Friend,
    Thanks for the food Thy love doth send,
As we, Thy bounties now partake,
    Make us anew for Thy son's sake.   Amen.

✠

June 18

Thou art so constant in Thy devotion, O
Lord, that we come to this table to accept
another manifestation of Thy love with hearts
filled with humiliation—ashamed that in
accepting all Thy gifts we have, through our
spiritual weakness, returned nothing in duty
to Thee and our fellow-man.   Help us to see
the Light which Thou hast told us to spread
"far and wide," that not only ourselves but all
others will have the blessing of our Holy
Father.   Amen.

June 19

We thank Thee, our Father, for Thy many blessings. Sanctify this food to our good and save us, for Christ's sake. Amen.

✠

June 20

Father, make us thankful for all Thy blessings, grant us Thy presence from day to day, and sustain us for Thy service, in the name of our Blessed Redeemer. Amen.

✠

June 21

Pardon our past offences, Father, and make us truly thankful for these and all other blessings, for Christ's sake. Amen.

June 22

We give thanks unto Thee, Heavenly Father, for these many blessings. Teach us the good in life and our duty to Thee. Forgive us our sins, and bring us to eternal life. Amen.

✠

June 23

For the dear Saviour's sake, bless, O God, we beseech Thee this provision of Thy bounty to our use and ourselves to Thy service, and give us grace to enjoy and be thankful for these and all Thy mercies. Amen.

✠

June 24

Our merciful Father, accept our humble thanks for this bread placed before us. Realizing our unworthiness of Thine untold ` love, we desire to serve Thee better to-day than yesterday, to-morrow than to-day. Keep us faithful and save us at last in heaven. Amen.

June 25

O Lord grant us heavenly wisdom that we may learn above all things to seek and find Thee, to cherish and love Thee, and in all to yield Thee submissive obedience. We praise Thee for all Thy love, and for the blessings before us spread. Amen.

✠

June 26

Dear Saviour, be our guest to-day in all we do or say, bless Thou the food that is set before us, and may Thy loving care watch over us. Amen.

✠

June 27

O God, we are grateful to Thee for these temporal gifts. How grateful we should be for the gift of gifts, our Saviour Jesus Christ, to whom be all glory. Amen.

June 28

We praise Thee, Father, for the spiritual food Thou dost give us, and also for this our daily bread, wherewith our bodies are sustained. Help us to grow, as in body, so in spirit, into all strength, through Christ. Amen.

✠

June 29

With gratitude we acknowledge these gifts and all the benefits of Thy grace. Help us to live for Thy glory through Jesus Christ our Lord. Amen.

✠

June 30

Our Heavenly Father, we thank Thee for all Thy mercies. Give the sanctified use of this food and forgive our sins, we ask through Christ. Amen.

July

July 1

Lord, Thy protecting arm is all about us. May we ever nestle close to Thee and trust in Thee. Feed us in body and in soul from Thy hand, and save us in heaven. Amen.

✠

July 2

In our life and health, O Lord, we see Thy gifts. Forbid that we should use Thy gifts without regard to Thee, but rather as just stewards. For Christ's sake. Amen.

✠

July 3

O Lord, we are glad to meet once more at this table Thou hast spread for us. Abide with those who are usually with us at this time. Strengthen us and them, and grant that we may be united, if not by Thy will on earth, at last in Heaven for Jesus' sake. Amen.

July 4

Independence Day.

We ask Thy blessing to-day upon this glorious Republic. Shield her from error, guard her from corruption, make of her a nation after Thine own heart. For the liberty whose birthday we celebrate to-day, we give Thee gracious thanks, especially for the liberty of serving Thee according as Thou dost give us wisdom. Vouchsafe Thy continued providence over us, and eventually may we be gathered at Thy right hand in glory. Amen.

✠

July 5

We give Thee thanks, Heavenly Father, for every evidence of Thy love. Supply unto us all that Thou knowest that we stand in need of. Help us to be grateful to Thee. Amen.

✠

July 6

We thank Thee, dear Lord, for this food. Bless it to the use of our perishing bodies, and us to Thy service, we ask for Christ's sake. Amen.

July 7

Bless to our good this food which Thou hast given human hands the power to place before us. May we always give Thee the glory of all that is ours, and when we have served Thee well on earth may we in Heaven hear Thy "Well done, thou good and faithful servant." Amen.

✠

July 8

Our Father we thank Thee for this food. Bless it to our good and give of Thy bounty to the poor and needy. We ask it in the name of our Saviour. Amen.

✠

July 9

O taste and see that the Lord is good, blessed is the man that trusteth in Him. May we trust in the Lord and do good, so shall we dwell in His presence and verily we shall be fed. Amen.

July 10

Most Holy and Kind Father, we as unworthy servants do approach Thee again with our thanks for the many blessings that Thou hast bestowed upon us, and for the daily bread Thou hast provided for us. We remember, dear Lord, that Thou hast said that we can not live by bread alone, but by every word of God. Amen.

✠

July 11

O give thanks unto the God of Heaven who giveth food to all flesh, for his mercy endureth forever. The Lord will give strength unto His people; the Lord will bless His people with peace. Amen.

✠

July 12

Bless us, Lord, this day and go Thou with us through all its hours. As we take this food from Thy hand, may we also receive from Thee the word of life to-day. Amen.

July 13

We give Thee thanks, Almighty Father, for all these Thy graces to us, who are but the creatures of sin. Unto Thee we look for every earthly good, and for eternal salvation. Through Jesus Christ our Lord. Amen.

✠

July 14

It is a good thing to give thanks unto the Lord and to sing praise unto Thy name, O Most High, to show forth Thy loving kindness in the morning and Thy faithfulness every night. Amen.

✠

July 15

Help us, O God of our salvation, for the glory of Thy name, provide our daily food, and purge away our sins. So we, Thy people and sheep of Thy pasture, will give Thee thanks forever. Amen.

July 16

We thank Thee, O Lord, for the blessings Thou hast placed upon This food so generously provided from Thy bounty. May we never fail to help our fellow-man as Thou helpest us and bear in mind always that this is a part of Thy teaching. Amen.

✠

July 17

For the dear Saviour's sake, bless, O God, this provision of Thy bounty to our use, and ourselves to Thy service. Give us grace to relish and appreciate these and all Thy mercies. Through Christ. Amen.

✠

July 18

By day, by night, at home, abroad,
Still are we guided by our God;
By His incessant bounty fed,
By His unerring counsel led. Amen.

July 19

Again we are brought to a realization of the great love Thou hast for Thy weak children in the provision of this food Thou dost place before us. Always make us grateful for Thy love and mercies and save our souls for Christ's sake. Amen.

✠

July 20

We love Thee, O Christ, because Thou hast first loved us. Make our lives living epistles, telling forth our thankfulness for all the evidences of Thy great Heart of Love. Continue with and in us and bless this meal. For Thy name's sake. Amen.

✠

July 21

Give us this day Thy Holy Spirit that in body and in spirit we may be Thine indeed. Grant us to be continually thankful for these favors before us, and all Thy countless mercies, through Jesus Christ, Thy Son, Our Lord. Amen.

July 22

Strengthen us, O God, by the grace of Thy Holy Spirit. Grant us to be strong within, and to empty our hearts of all that encumbers. May we continue in thankfulness to look up unto Thee, who givest bread to the hungry. Through Christ Jesus. Amen.

✠

July 23

In the midst of life's occupations we come together around this table which Thou, O Lord, hast covered with Thy providing love. Help us to return to Thee always the good gift of gratitude, for Thine is all glory. Amen.

✠

July 24

O Lord Jesus, erase the record of our wrongs by Thy cleansing power. Glorify Thyself wherein we may have pleased Thee. Come Thou with us here and now and so make us worthy to sit at meat with Thee. Amen.

July 25

O God, Thou art the refuge of the weary, the strength of the weak. Give us this day the faith to nestle to Thy heart that throbs for us, and to feed in peace and confidence from the abundance of Thy hand. Through our Saviour Christ. Amen.

✠

July 26

We bless Thee, our Father, for new strength every day, and for these present tokens of Thy love. May we receive them with true gratitude and go forth to use them in Thy service. For Christ's sake. Amen.

✠

July 27

Lord, Thou art ever ready to shower blessings upon Thy children. We glorify Thee for this food, to us the earnest of Thy care over us. Through the hours of labor or pleasure help us to remember Thee ever. Amen.

July 28

Grant, O Christ, that we may worthily feast at Thy table here and be accounted worthy through Thy grace to be admitted to Thy table hereafter, at the eternal supper of the Lamb, and to Thee, Father, Son, and Holy Spirit, be glory and honor. Amen.

☩

July 29

With the coming of this day, O God, we acknowledge fresh tokens of Thy love. Grace Thou this house with Thy presence, and break with us the bread of life. In the name of Jesus. Amen.

☩

July 30

Wherein we have failed to please Thee, O God, do Thou grant Thy pardon. We praise Thee for all the good we have received, especially for these present blessings. Through Christ our Saviour. Amen.

Our Father, we ask Thy blessing upon us as we partake of this bountiful provision, for which we give Thee thanks. Make us faithful workers for Thee and forgive all our transgressions. We ask it in the name of our Redeemer. Amen.

August

August 1

O God, may the blessings which Thou givest us minister to health, holiness and thanksgiving and in the strength of Thy provisions may we cheerfully and diligently serve Thee. We ask this in Jesus' name. Amen.

✠

August 2

Our Heavenly Father, we thank Thee for these and all other blessings. Consecrate them to our good, keep us ever faithful in Thy service and forgive us our sins. In Jesus' name we ask it. Amen.

✠

August 3

As Thou hast kept us through the days gone by and provided all our bodily needs, so, O Lord, may Thy constant care guard us from all harm and still give us our daily bread. To Thee is all glory and thanksgiving. Amen.

August 4

Thou, O Lord, art the fountain of life eternal. Give us all grace to trust Thee for our refreshing. May we find joy in Thy presence, and strength of body and soul in Thine abundant blessing. Amen.

✠

August 5

We thank Thee, Almighty God, for this timely bread for our perishing bodies. Give unto us also the Bread of Heaven, that we may lay hold of the life that is forever. For Christ's sake. Amen.

✠

August 6

Why do we, O Lord, receive so much from Thee and give so little. Help us that we may return to Thee, that we may turn from sin and do Thy bidding. Accept our humble gratitude for these continued blessings and save us for Christ's sake. Amen.

August 7

Thou, O God, from whom all blessings flow, accept our humble thanks for this food, which we so weak and so frail do need. Let it impart to us health and strength which may be used in Thy work. Amen.

✠

August 8

Guide us, Lord, by Thy Holy Spirit, that we may know Thy truth, feel Thy light, drink of the living water and eat of the bread of Heaven. And to Thee be glory forever and ever. Amen.

▨

August 9

We do thank Thee, O Saviour, for these blessings and pray to Thee that Thou wilt help us to resist the temptations that claim us at times for sin. May we do better in the future and give thanks to Thee for the mercies constantly shown us. Amen.

August 10

We are most grateful to Thee, O Lord, for these other evidences of Thy care and love. Help us that we may never stray from the paths of the righteous and that we may always do Thy bidding. Amen.

✠

August 11

Thy blessings do impress us, O Lord, with Thy great love for us. Let us always have the courage to acknowledge Thee and to make ourselves more worthy of Thy great mercies. Amen.

✠

August 12

Once more we thank Thee, blessed Saviour, as we come with grateful hearts to the blessings which are before us. Grant us divine grace, Lord, ever to live for Thee and to refrain from sin and wrong, for Thy dear name's sake. Amen.

August 13

Accept our thanks, O Lord, for this food which Thou, through Thy great love for us do provide. Forgive us our sins and save us for Christ's sake. Amen.

✠

August 14

Gracious God, we thank Thee for all Thy mercy, love and goodness. Grant Thy blessing unto those who are not so favored as we, and help us to be faithful in return for all Thy mercies. Amen.

✠

August 15

We bless Thee, O God, for this food which betokens Thy continued care over us; we acknowledge this gift, and Thy love which prompts it, and pray for fidelity to use our strength in doing Thy good pleasure, for Jesus' sake. Amen.

August 16

Make us truly grateful, Our Father, for the blessings we are about to receive, and enable us to see in them another evidence of Thy constant care and love.   Amen.

✠

August 17

Accept, O Father, our humble thanks for this our daily food, and as it adds strength to our mortal bodies, may it give us power to render better service to Thee, in Christ's name. Amen.

✠

August 18

O Lord, through this food grant unto us bodily health and spiritual power. Bless these hearts united in Thy praise, and may we eventually sit together at the marriage supper of Thy dear Son, in whose name we ask it.   Amen.

August 19

Lord, may we thank Thee acceptably. Bless Thou this food to its intended use, and make us useful servants of Thine, for the Christ's sake. Amen.

✠

August 20

We thank Thee, dear Lord, for our daily bread. Consecrate it to the upbuilding of our perishing bodies, and us to the upbuilding of Thy kingdom. We ask it for Jesus' sake. Amen.

✠

August 21

Indulgent Heavenly Father, we thank Thee for these daily refreshments from Thy bountiful hand, and for every expression of Thy goodness manifested toward us. Pardon our unworthiness, we ask in the name of Christ. Amen.

August 22

Lord, we thank Thee for this Thy bountiful provision. Feed us ever on the bodily bread, and on the Bread of our souls, that we may be made strong in body and soul to do Thy will. Amen.

☩

August 23

In coming together, Lord, to be fed from Thy hand, we acknowledge that through Thee all our daily needs are supplied. Give us the grace to be grateful, and to continue to walk in the paths of righteousness, for Thy name's sake. Amen.

☩

August 24

Our Father, we thank Thee for the manifestations of Thy love to us in Jesus Christ. Help us to live to His praise and be pleased to sanctify these temporal blessings to our nourishment, we ask in His name. Amen.

August 25

Dear Father, for these bounties of Thy love, and for the communion we have together with Thee we give Thee thanks. In all these things make Thy name glorious, for Christ's sake. Amen.

✠

August 26

Lord, hear our prayer of thanksgiving for every blessing which we have received. Pardon all our wrongs, and watch over us, for the Saviour's sake. Amen.

✠

August 27

O Gracious Father, Thou knowest how much our health, strength and happiness depend on our food. We thank Thee for these blessings of Thy providence. May we always love and serve Thee as Thou hast loved us, for Jesus' sake. Amen.

August 28

Dear Jesus, as Thou dost break the bread of bodily nourishment unto us, grant that we may likewise partake of the Bread of Life broken for us on Mount Calvary. Amen.

✠

August 29

For this and every expression of Thy great love we are profoundly thankful, O God. Give us the vision to discern all Thy blessings, and fill us with gratitude. Amen.

✠

August 30

For life, health and strength and these blessings and mercies which we receive constantly from Thy hand, accept our thanks O Lord. We are grateful for this food. We pray that it may be used to Thy honor. Amen.

August 31

Blessed Lord, we are daily refreshed from the bounty of Thy store house. Bless our portion to-day, and give us grateful hearts. Amen.

September

Labor Day

As we ask Thy blessing upon our home to-day, we ask too that Thou wilt graciously bless the home of all those who live by the sweat of their brow. Give us the health to labor on, and grace to be proud of labor, remembering the example of our Lord, and his word of commendation that the laborer is worthy of his hire. Continue with us this day and evermore. Amen.

✠

September 1

O Lord, our Shepherd, Thou hast not suffered us to come to want. Thou hast prepared the way of peace and plenty before us. May we still give to Thee all thanks, in Jesus' name. Amen.

September 2

O Lord, Thou art most gracious and provideth for all our needs. Let the mercies
Thou art always showing descend upon all.
Make us always grateful for the provision of
our food, and save us from sin, in Jesus'
name. Amen.

✠

September 3

Gracious Father, we praise Thy mercy
which provides so faithfully for us. By this
food make us stronger in body and mind, in
order that we may draw nearer to Thyself,
for Christ's sake. Amen.

✠

September 4

Grant, we beseech Thee O Lord, Thy blessing upon this provision of Thy bounty to our
use, keep us ever faithful and constant in
Thy service and pardon our sins. Amen.

September 5

O Heavenly Father, for our daily bread and the manifold blessings Thou showest us we are deeply grateful. Strengthen us that we may resist all temptations and live the clean, pure life in which we have been enlightened. Forgive us our sins and save us, for Christ's sake. Amen.

September 6

In Thy goodness, O God, Thou hast made provision for Thy many poor. We are constantly dependent upon Thee for our food. Help us as we eat to bless Thee, the Giver of every good gift. Amen.

September 7

Transform this food into life, O God, and transform that life into useful service of Thee, for Jesus' sake. Amen.

September 8

The blessings we receive from Thee, O Lord, each day are a token of Thy great love. We ask Thee to make us strong and healthy, and that we may do Thy work and be received in the Kingdom of Heaven. Accept our thanks for this food and grant that we may continue to receive Thy bounties. Amen.

✠

September 9

We bless Thee O God, for the privilege of receiving these bounties from Thy hand. Use them to our good and purify our hearts from all sin. We ask it in His name. Amen.

✠

September 10

For this, our daily bread, and for every good gift which cometh down from Thee, we bless Thy holy name through Jesus Christ our Lord. Amen.

September 11

Lord, another day has brought forth fresh tokens of Thy great love to us. Bless the opportunities of this day, and the food wherewith we are made strong to serve Thee. These and all favors we ask in Jesus' name. Amen.

✠

September 12

Lord, Thou alone knowest what is good for us. Do unto us what seemeth Thee best, and grant that in humble gratitude and submission we may receive Thy providence and render Thee our ceaseless thanks. Through Jesus Christ our Lord. Amen.

✠

September 13

Our constant and expectant faith, O Lord, finds its ready answer in Thy daily mercies to us, Thy children. Bless us with grateful hearts, for Jesus' sake. Amen.

September 14

This bread we eat, O Lord, is but the shadow of that other bread of Thine. May we also partake of that truer bread, which cometh down from Heaven, Thy Son Jesus Christ. Amen.

✠

September 15

Once more, O Lord, we dedicate to Thee our power of body and mind. Sanctify them and refresh them with these present blessings. May we never grow weary in well-doing, but be fervent in spirit, and fruitful in service. Through Christ our Saviour. Amen.

✠

September 16

Lord, Thou hast created us, Thou hast brought us back from sin, Thou hast fed us out of Thine own hand. Bless us to-day, and keep us Thine forevermore. Amen.

September 17

This food which Thou hast already blessed in the giving, do Thou further bless in our partaking, that it may redound to Thy Glory, in Christ's name.   Amen.

✠

September 18

Let Thy manifold blessings fix such lasting impressions upon our souls, O God, that we may always praise Thee faithfully on earth, until it shall please Thee, of Thy unbounded mercy, to call us nearer to the place of Thy heavenly habitation to praise our Lord and Deliverer to all eternity.   Amen.

✠

September 19

Lord God, we rejoice to attribute unto Thee every good and perfect gift. For these present expressions of Thy grace accept our deep thanks.   Amen.

September 20

Lord, as we, Thy grateful children approach Thy table, bless this food in the using, and cleanse us of all sin, through the Christ. Amen.

✠

September 21

Help us to trust always to Thy goodness, O Lord, knowing that Thou wilt keep him in perfect peace whose mind is stayed on Thee. May we learn in whatsoever state we are placed by Thy providence, therewith to be content. Bless us continually as Thou seest we have need. Amen.

✠

September 22

Thy gifts toward us speak fervently of Thy love. Grant, Lord, that we by our lives may in some small measure bespeak the gratitude that is within us, through Jesus Christ. Amen.

September 23

We thank Thee that through Thy mercy strength and health are given unto us. May we use every gift as faithful stewards of Thine and finally hear Thy heavenly greeting, "Well done, good and faithful servant; enter thou into the joys of thy Lord." Amen.

✠

September 24

Dear Saviour, Thou hast kept us from harm and given us strength sufficient for our day. To Thee be praise forevermore. We give Thee thanks to-day for life and health, for the comfort of our home, and for the food Thou hast set before us. Amen.

✠

September 25

It is with grateful hearts that we remember Thy constant mercies, O Lord. Help us so to live as to glorify Thy holy name, through Christ our Redeemer. Amen.

September 26

Lord, make us thankful for this food and wherein the flesh is weak, make us strong. Pardon us our many sins and save our souls. Amen.

✠

September 27

May no thought of earth and its manifold cares tempt us, O Father, to forget Thee. Remind us now through these graces that Thou ever lovest and carest for Thine own. Help us to be as constant in our praise and obedience to Thee. Amen.

✠

September 28

We acknowledge our gratitude to Thee for all good gifts, O Father. In our use of them may we prove that Thy trust has been well bestowed. For the blessed name of Jesus we pray. Amen.

September 29

Lord, Thy mercies and favors are without number. Make us more worthy to be the recipients of Thy grace, and pardon all that Thou seest amiss in us, for Jesus' sake.   Amen.

✠

September 30

Almighty God, and gracious Father of men, who openest Thy hand and fillest all things with plenty, and hast provided Thy children sufficient to satisfy all our need, teach us to render back to Thee Thy due thanksgiving, not only in words, but also in the manner of our living. For Christ's sake. Amen.

October

October 1

We thank Thee, Lord, for this our food,
But more because of Jesus' blood.
Let manna to our souls be given,
The Bread of Life, sent down from heaven.

Amen.

✠

October 2

Lord, Thou hast not need of our thanks, but we have daily need to remind ourselves of our obligation unto Thee. For all Thy mercies make us ever truly grateful. Amen.

✠

October 3

O God, the Father of lights from whom cometh down every good and perfect gift; mercifully look down upon our frailty, and grant unto us such sustenance as Thou knowest to be needful for us. In body and soul may we ever serve Thee with all love and gratitude. Amen.

October 4

Be Thou the silent guest of this our home. Fill us with Thy sweet temper, that whether we eat, or whether we drink, or whatsoever we do, all may be done as to the Lord.   Amen.

✠

October 5

We thank Thee that Thou art a God that hearest and answerest prayer. We thank Thee that Thou hast given unto us exceeding abundantly, more than we could ask or think. So help us to be unstinted in our loving obedience to Thee.   Amen.

✠

October 6

We thank Thee, O Lord, for Thy hidden blessings, and for those we may have passed over in neglect or thoughtlessness.   We thank Thee for a Saviour's love and a Father's providing care.   Guard us from ingratitude and glorify Thyself in us.   For Christ's sake.   Amen.

October 7

Give unto us health and strength to enjoy Thy daily blessings, Lord. Fulfil our present need, we pray Thee, and pardon our sins. Amen.

✠

October 8

Father, hear us while we pray,
　　Look in mercy from above.
Give us health and strength to-day,
　　Hear and grant Thy pardoning love.
　　　　　　　　　　　　Amen.

✠

October 9

Praise to God, immortal praise,
For the love that crowns our days;
Bounteous source of every joy!
Let Thy praise our tongues employ;
All to Thee our God we owe.
Source whence all our blessings flow.
　　　　　　　　　　　　Amen.

October 10

Lord, we have need of strong bodies and alert minds. Through Thy daily supply of blessings, grant us these and help us to consecrate them to Thee. In Jesus' name hear us. Amen.

✠

October 11

We thank Thee, Father, that in loving Thy children, Thou dost care for their daily needs. Engender in us the spirit of childlike faith, as we ask in Jesus' name. Amen.

✠

October 12

It is a great blessing, O Lord, to receive daily these tokens of Thy love. This food, this life, are instruments through which Thou dost manifest Thy eternal love. May we be worthy of it and serve Thee faithfully and work constantly for Thy cause. Amen.

October 13

We thank our Lord to-day for His past and present blessing. May we never forget Thee as the source of all we need. Bless us always, in Christ's name. Amen.

✠

October 14

May the Holy Spirit abide with us as we partake of these comforts. Make us this day more willing to follow our Lord and take up our cross for Him. Amen.

✠

October 15

If Thou wilt accept our thanks, O God, for this food and our prayer for the forgiveness of our sins, do so and give us the spirit, the determination and the courage to live up to better ideals, ideals that will influence others with whom we are associated to do better, and that we may set for ourselves a standard from which we will never depart. Amen.

October 16

Father, who hast loved this poor world, make us grateful for Thy gifts and above all else for the Gift of Love, Thy Son Jesus Christ. May we be counted among those who by their belief on Him inherit eternal life. Amen.

✠

October 17

Every day we receive from Thy hand that which shows Thy love for our life. Make us worthy to live, by ever living worthily, and to Thy name shall be the glory. Amen.

✠

October 18

Help us, O Lord, to be more grateful for Thy blessings and the food which Thou dost provide for us each day. We are not always as thoughtful as we should be; we acknowledge our sins and pray that we may be given the grace of God to be better and set a better example for those whom our actions and words might influence. Amen.

October 19

O Lord, our Shepherd, make us to lie down in green pastures of full trust in Thee; lead us by the still waters of Thy refreshing grace; restore Thou our souls, and lead us in the paths of righteousness, for Thy name's sake. Amen.

☩

October 20

As our want and penury returns upon us, O Lord, so frequent is the return of Thy grace. Fill the mouths of Thy children, bless the poor, and continue Thy protecting care over us all, for Jesus' sake.   Amen.

☩

October 21

For the great mercies shown us, O Lord, we pray that Thou wilt show us the light that we may not be cast upon the rocks of wickedness.   Help us ever to be grateful for these bounties and the food before us and that we may help others to do all that is best.   Amen.

October 22

Our Mighty God, Thou hast supplied us with
the bounties of life, and for these our hearts
go out in gratitude to Thee. Bless us continually as we hold out our empty hands for
Thee to fill. In Christ's name. Amen.

✠

October 23

Countless are Thy blessings, Lord. We
have need to be thanking Thee moment by
moment for all Thy goodness. We praise
Thee now for these table blessings, and
acknowledge that all our good cometh from
Thee. Amen.

✠

October 24

In the manifestation of Thy great love for
us, O Lord, we come to ask that Thou provideth
also for the needy and poor even though our
own share be diminished. Let not our faith in
Thee be shaken, as from this we gain the
greatest benefits. Accept our thanks for
this food and save us for Christ's sake. Amen.

October 25

Strengthen us by these material gifts, O Lord, that we may have that more abundant life which Thou didst come to give us. Help us to use that life for the glory of Thy kingdom, for Thy name's sake. Amen.

✠

October 26

Heavenly Father, break unto us to-day the Bread of Life; cleanse our hearts from sin, and every evil thought to which we are prone. Do good to us in Thy good pleasure, and renew a right spirit in us. Give us this day our daily bread. Amen.

✠

October 27

It is with profoundly grateful hearts we come to Thee, O Lord, to offer thanks for this food which Thou so faithfully and constantly provideth to nourish our bodies. May we use it to Thy good and may our love and service for Thee ever increase. Amen.

October 28

It is Thou, O Lord, who hast given all our increase. Thou sendest rain and sunshine, health and prosperity. We thank Thee for what we enjoy, and beseech Thy constant protection for ourselves and our loved ones. Amen.

☩

October 29

Let Thy providing grace seek out the needy, the poor and the sorrowful, Lord. As we partake, may we feel that Thy watch care is over those less favored than ourselves. Deliver us from all selfishness, and make us like unto Thee, through Christ. Amen.

☩

October 30

We do come unto Thee again, O Lord, with grateful hearts to offer our thanks for Thy great mercies and the food which Thou dost provide for us daily to nourish our bodies. May we use the strength thus gained for Thy cause and bring others unto Thee to offer their thanks. Amen.

October 31

According unto the multitude of Thy tender mercies, O God, blot out the record of our sins. Create within us clean hearts and imbue us with thankfulness for Thy continued mercies, through Jesus Christ. Amen.

November

November 1

The earth is Thine, O God. Grant in Thy love to survey the broad expanse of Thy dominion, and this day bless our loved ones. Provide for their needs as ours, and watch between us and them while we are absent one from the other. Amen.

✠

November 2

O Thou Merciful God, as Thou dost provide us each day with the necessities of the life which Thou hast so graciously given us, pardon our sins in the past and save us from them in the future. May this prayer be heard as our other prayers have been, and our thanks be accepted for this food which Thou hast again placed before us. Amen.

✠

November 3

Guide us by Thy spirit into all the truth as it is in Christ Jesus, prepare us to receive these daily graces in the spirit of thankfulness, and lead us eventually to our home in Heaven with Thee Amen.

November 4

Dear Lord, accept our sincere thanks for these new blessings, and hear us in our prayer for pardon. In Jesus' name we ask Thee. Amen.

✠

November 5

O Lord, forgive our sins in the past and those we may commit in the future, but help us to avoid temptation that we may not fall, that we may lead a proper life and make it useful to Thee and our fellow-man. We give Thee thanks for this provision of food from Thy bounty, and pray that Thy mercies may be continued. Amen.

✠

November 6

We read in every providence of Thy love and watch care. May all things work together for our good, according as we love Thee. Amen.

November 7

Remind us, Lord, from day to day of our continued dependence upon Thee, and enable us with thanksgiving to receive Thine every blessing. Amen.

✠

November 8

If, in all these years through which we have been permitted to enjoy the life Thou hast given us, we have failed to remember Thee and what Thou hast done for us, forgive us, O Lord, and accept our prayer. Accept our thanks for this, another day of Thy great mercy and love and bless this food to Thy use. Amen.

✠

November 9

Enable us, O Christ, to devote our lives fully to Thee, in return for all Thy daily mercies. Sanctify these gifts to their intended uses, and purge our souls from sin by Thine own blood. Amen.

November 10

Lord, Thou didst crown Thy creative works by making man in Thine image, and dedicating unto his use all the products of the ground. May Thy trust not be betrayed. May we use these blessings as in Thy sight, and render to Thee true gratitude. Amen.

✠

November 11

We must return to Thee something, O Lord, for Thy great love for us. We accept daily Thy great mercies with wonder at the constancy of Thy love for creatures so weak and sinful. Help us to be strong that we may keep Thy commandments and in so doing help others to do Thy bidding. Amen.

✠

November 12

The strength of the hills, and the depth of the
    sea,
The earth and its fulness belongeth to Thee;
And yet to the lowly Thou bendest Thine ear,
So ready their humble petitions to hear.
Amen.

November 13

All honor and praise to Thine excellent name;
  Thy love is unchanging, forever the same;
We bless and adore Thee, O Saviour and King;
  With joy and thanksgiving Thy praises we
    sing.   Amen.

✠

November 14

Thou art full of love for us, O Lord, as Thou
showest us from day to day.   Let us show unto
our fellow-man the love which Thou teachest
and convey to him the light we have received
from Thee.   Accept this, our thanks, for the
food spread before us and help us to live a good
and useful life.   Amen.

✠

November 15

Remembering these and all Thy blessings,
Lord, help us to spend our best energies in
the advancement of that Kingdom which
Jesus came into the world to establish, and
may we enthrone Him in our own hearts first.
In His name.   Amen.

November 16

Bless, O Lord, this food to our use, and give us thankful hearts, through Jesus Christ our Lord. Amen.

✠

November 17

Dear Father, we give Thee thanks for life and health and for this our daily bread, that Thou hast given for our physical strength. Feed our souls, we pray Thee, with Thy Holy Spirit and finally bring us safely unto Thyself in glory, for Christ's sake. Amen.

✠

November 18

We are ever conscious, Lord, of our sinfulness and our constant need of Thee. Support our lives by Thy grace, and bring us safely to Thy heavenly home. Amen.

November 19

Cover all our sins with Thy pardon, O Christ, and make us strong to overcome all sins, especially the sin of ingratitude. In all these bounties help us to see Thee, and glorify Thee. Amen.

✠

November 20

Dear Father, hear the prayer of Thy children, that as we travel life's journey from day to day, thanking Thee ever, Thou wilt lead us on into that Great Country where our imperfect faith shall blossom into knowledge, and our feeble thanks shall give way to the hallelujahs of Heavenly praise. Amen.

✠

November 21

Be merciful, O God, to those in darkness and sin to-day. Lead them to the light, that they may see as we see Thy great love. Hasten the day when every nation shall return due thanks to Thee. Amen.

November 22

Thou hast not redeemed us for ourselves alone. Give us some share in Thy great plans of spreading abroad the Gospel of Salvation, and may that message show its power in our own lives. Amen.

✠

November 23

Thine infinite goodness our tongues shall
   employ;
Thou givest us richly all things to enjoy;
We'll follow Thy footsteps, we'll rest in Thy
   love,
And soon we shall praise Thee in mansions
   above. Amen.

✠

Thanksgiving Day

Once more we come, Lord, to the day of special thanksgiving. Our thoughts are turned backward. The days have rolled into the seasons, the seasons into the year. Each day has been crowded with Thee. Each season has brought forth new proofs of Thy loving forethought. May we this day pledge Thee our gratitude anew. Continue, we pray Thee, to surround us with Thy care, in Jesus' name. Amen.

November 24

Our Father who art in Heaven, we thank Thee for blessings, enjoyments, powers afforded unto us and unto all men, and for all good that has been given to this generation in its manifold forms. Help us to realize how many greater and better things God has waiting for us, and accordingly to glorify His name. Amen.

✠

November 25

Lord, Thou art a fountain that never faileth. Fail us not in this, our physical need. Above all else, help us to call on Thee for the daily supply of spiritual power we need. Through Christ. Amen.

✠

November 26

Reveal unto us more of Thyself, O God, that we may know more of Thy love, and be yet more conscious that Thou art the giver of every good and perfect gift. Accept our thanks, and grant us Thy salvation. Amen.

November 27

We ask Thy blessing upon the meal now spread before us. Help us to feel more than we can of ourselves that all that we have cometh from Thee. Strengthen us by these material things that we may serve Thee better in spirit and in true holiness of life. In the name of the Great Three in One. Amen.

✠

November 28

Heavenly Father, we thank Thee for this food; as it nourishes the body may it strengthen us in Thy service. Amen.

✠

November 29

Dear Lord make us truly thankful for blessings we are about to receive, which are another manifestation of the great mercy and love shown us by our Saviour. Amen.

Most gracious God we thank Thee for Thy mercy, goodness and love. We thank Thee for this food. Remember those who are not so fortunate as we and grant that we shall be faithful in return for all these mercies, for Christ's sake. Amen.

December

December 1

We thank Thee dear Lord for this food.
Bless it to the nourishment of our perishing
bodies and us to Thy service, we ask for
Jesus' sake.   Amen.

✠

December 2

Heavenly Father, we give thanks to Thee.
Be with us during this meal and make us
more faithful to the One who taught us to
say: "Give us this day our daily bread."
Amen.

✠

December 3

We do thank Thee again, blessed Saviour,
and we do come with grateful hearts to the
blessings which Thou hast spread before us.
Grant us, Lord, Thy grace divine; help us
to live for Thee always, keep us free from
sin and wrong, and may our hearts be wholly
Thine, for Thy blessed name's sake.   Amen.

December 4

Accept our thanks for these blessings O Lord, and consecrate them to our use and us to Thy service, we ask in the name of our Saviour. Amen.

✠

December 5

As the Pilgrim lifted up his thanks to Thee, so lift we up our praise for the many blessings sent us. Amen

✠

December 6

We thank Thee, Father, for life and health and for this our daily food, that Thou hast given us to nourish these mortal bodies. Now we beseech Thee to feed our souls with Thy Holy Spirit and finally gather us into Thy Kingdom in one happy and unbroken family, for Christ's sake. Amen.

December 7

We are grateful unto Thee, O Father, for this material expression of Thy love. Open our eyes to see wherein Thou hast blessed us spiritually and make us thankful. Amen.

✠

December 8

Accept our thanks, O gracious Lord, for this food and for all the material and spiritual blessings we receive. Forgive our sins and watch over us in Jesus' name. Amen.

✠

December 9

As we come to Thy table, O Lord, to receive Thy favors we feel that Thou art the one and only God that can give us the Bread of Life forever. Accept our thanks, O Lord, and help us to walk in the paths of the righteous. Amen.

December 10

Our Father, we return thanks to Thee for
this bounty of Thy love and for the sweet
fellowship we have together. Sanctify it all
\ to Thy glory, we ask in Jesus' name. Amen.

✠

December 11

Blessed Master, as Thou didst sit at meat
with Thy disciples in Galilee, so be our spiritual
host and break the Bread of Life to us. Amen.

✠

December 12

Dear Lord, we thank Thee for the food
Thou hast provided for us. May we always
be able to have our daily bread and the
Bread of Life, and may we be given the
strength to serve Thee faithfully and work
for Thy cause. Amen.

December 13

Our Father, we give thanks to Thee for the returning day; for refreshed bodies; for these provisions of Thy love. Sanctify them all to Thy glory. Amen.

✠

December 14

O Lord, our Father, we thank Thee for another day of opportunity and for this physical nourishment. Feed our souls with Thy fellowship this day. Amen.

✠

December 15

Gracious Lord, Thou art breaking the bread of physical life to us. We thank Thee. Grant that our souls may feed upon Thy Son's flesh and blood given on Calvary. Amen.

December 16

Most gracious Lord from whose store house all are fed, bless we pray Thee, this our meal, for Jesus' sake. Amen.

✠

December 17

Sanctify this food, O Lord, that it may be life to the body, and use us in Thy service for Christ's sake. Amen.

✠

December 18

We give thanks to Thee, O Lord, that with the Psalmist each of us may say, "The Lord is my Shepherd, I shall not want" Bless this food and our fellowship to Thy glory, we ask in Jesus' name. Amen.

December 19

We are profoundly grateful, O God, for all Thy merciful kindness toward us. Accept our thanks for this food, and cleanse us from all sin, for Christ's sake. Amen.

✠

December 20

Our Heavenly Father, it is of Thy bounty we are fed. Bless this food to the strengthening of our bodies, and us to Thy service, for Christ's sake. Amen.

✠

December 21

O most merciful Father, we bless Thee for Thy great mercy in providing for our every need. May this food make stronger our bodies in order that we may more perfectly love Thee for Jesus' sake. Amen.

December 22

Thou, O God, hast of Thy goodness prepared for the poor. They shall eat and be satisfied and bless Thee—as we do this day. Amen.

✠

December 23

For our daily food, and all God's gifts His Holy Name be thanked and praised, through Jesus Christ our Lord. Amen.

✠

December 24

Dear Lord, we do gratefully thank Thee this day for allowing us the privilege of coming together again to enjoy the abundant blessing that Thou hast so lovingly provided for our physical bodies; may it be food for our bodies and nourishment for our souls, and may our hearts be made pure from all sin, for Jesus' sake. Amen.

Christmas
December 25—Morning

We thank Thee for the blessings received during the days that are gone, and ask Thy Divine blessing upon this food this Holy Christmas morning, for Jesus' sake. Amen.

✠

Christmas
December 25—Evening

We thank Thee for this day's feast, instituted by the Birth of Thy Holy Son. Bless us and guide us through all time, we ask for Jesus' sake. Amen.

✠

December 26

The eyes of all wait upon Thee, O Lord, and Thou givest them meat in due season. Amen.

December 27

Grant, O Lord, as we take this food with thankfulness, we may also receive the true Bread of Life—Thy son Jesus Christ our Lord. Amen.

✠

December 28

O Thou giver of every good and perfect gift, accept our tribute of praise, which we now offer, for this expression of Thy love to us, and this we ask on behalf of Christ our Saviour. Amen.

✠

December 29

Dear Lord, we thank Thee for this food. Sanctify it to the nourishment of our sinful bodies, pardon all our sins and save us in Heaven, for Christ's sake. Amen.

December 30

Our most merciful Father, who of gracious goodness hast heard the devout prayers of Thy church, and turned our dearth and scarcity into plenty, we give Thee humble thanks for this blessed food which Thou hast set before us. Through Jesus Christ Our Lord. Amen.

December 31

We thank Thee, Heavenly Father, for Thy love and mercies and that we are given the health and strength to lend our services to Thy work. Accept our great thanks for the food laid before us each day and Thy watchfulness and care over us. Help us to be always grateful for Thy mercies, forgive us our sins, and bring us to life everlasting. Amen.

Made in the USA
Monee, IL
28 September 2021